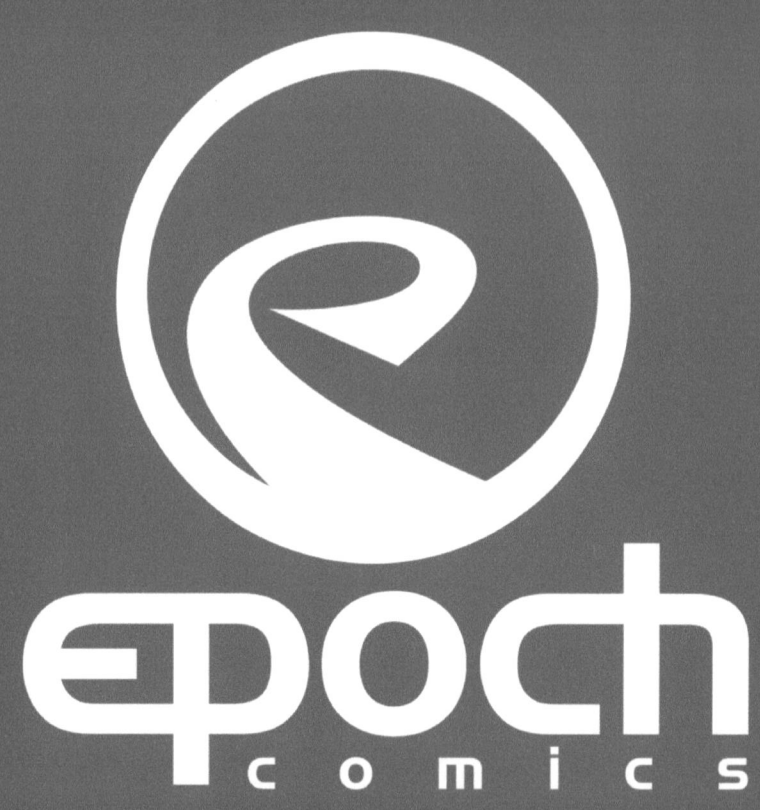

www.epochcomics.net

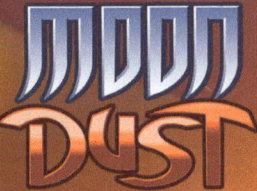

MOON DUST

CREATED BY
MARTIN OKONKWO,
EMMANUEL EZEABIAMA

ISSUE #2:
HERO AT LARGE

PENCILS / INKS
DOMINIC OZIREN OMOARUKHE

COLOURS
ABOSEDE AKANNI

SCRIPT
EMMANUEL EZEABIAMA

LETTERS / GRAPHICS
MARTIN OKONKWO

COVER ART / COLOURS
XAVIER SESOSE

PROJECT MANAGER
OGOO EZEOLU

VARIANT COVER
SUOYE EZEKIEL AREPAMOWEI

SPECIAL THANKS TO
David Ogbueli,
Ogochukwu Okonkwo
Emmanuel Mmadubuike
Dubus Achufusi

CEO
MARTIN
OKONKWO

CREATIVE DIRECTOR
EMMANUEL
EZEABIAMA

TECH
IKENNA
OKONKWO

PRODUCTS
JC. NOVA

STRATEGY & RISK
CHIMA EZEIBE

ADMIN / FINANCE
OGOO
EZEOLU

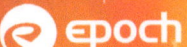 OCT 2023 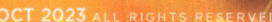 EPOCHCOMICS 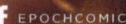 @EPOCHCOMICS_NG 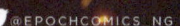 @EPOCHCOMICS

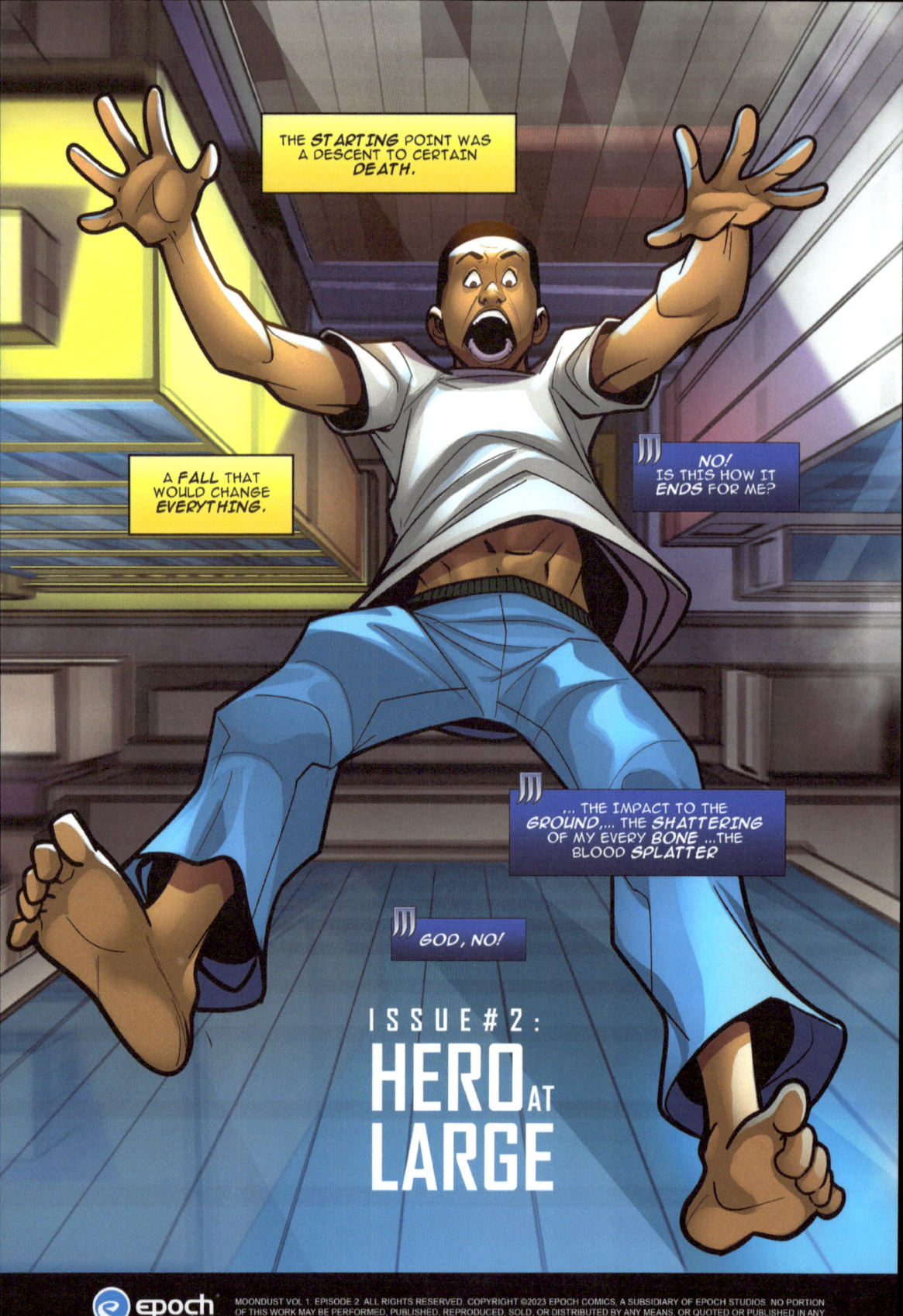

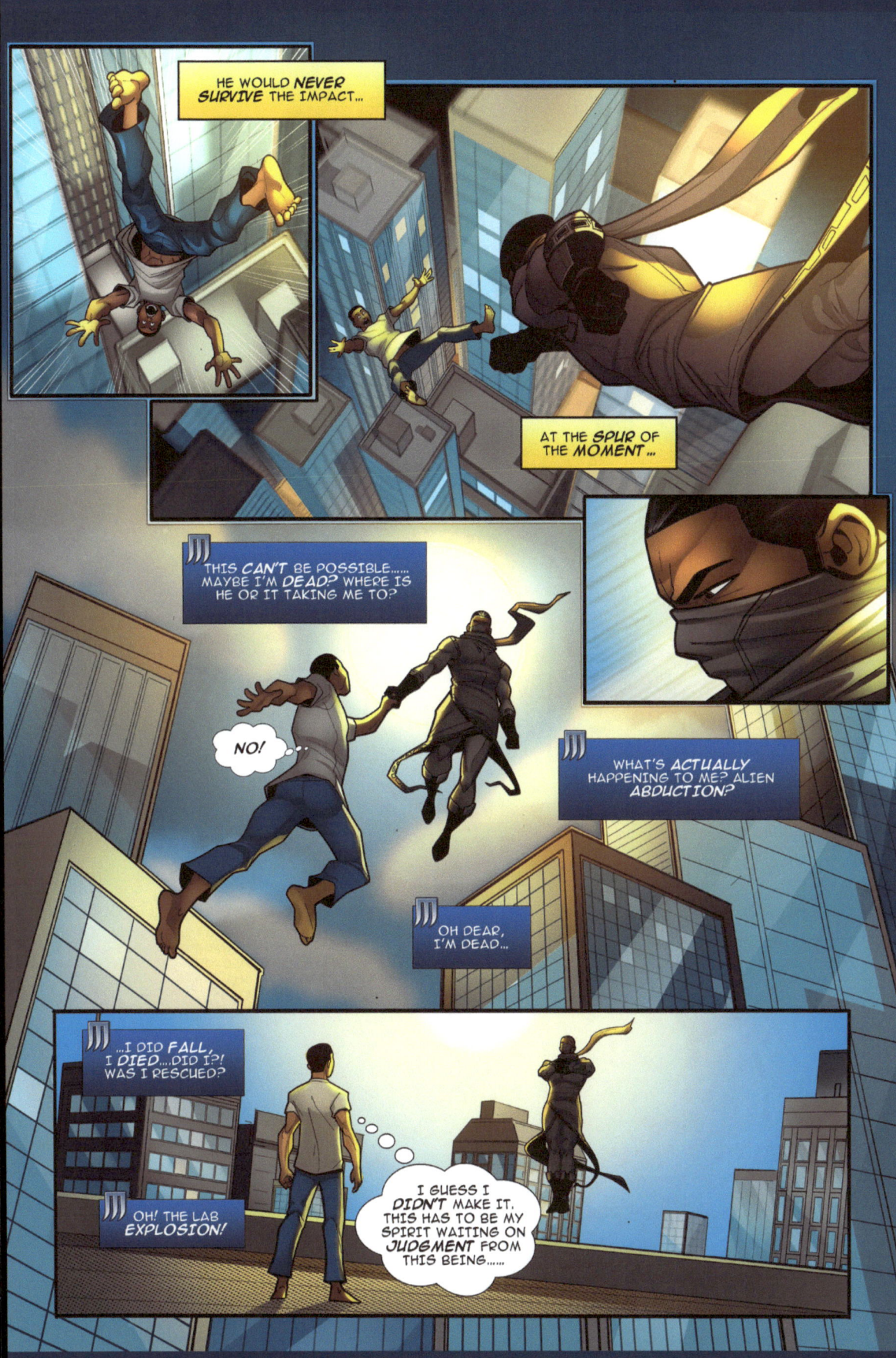

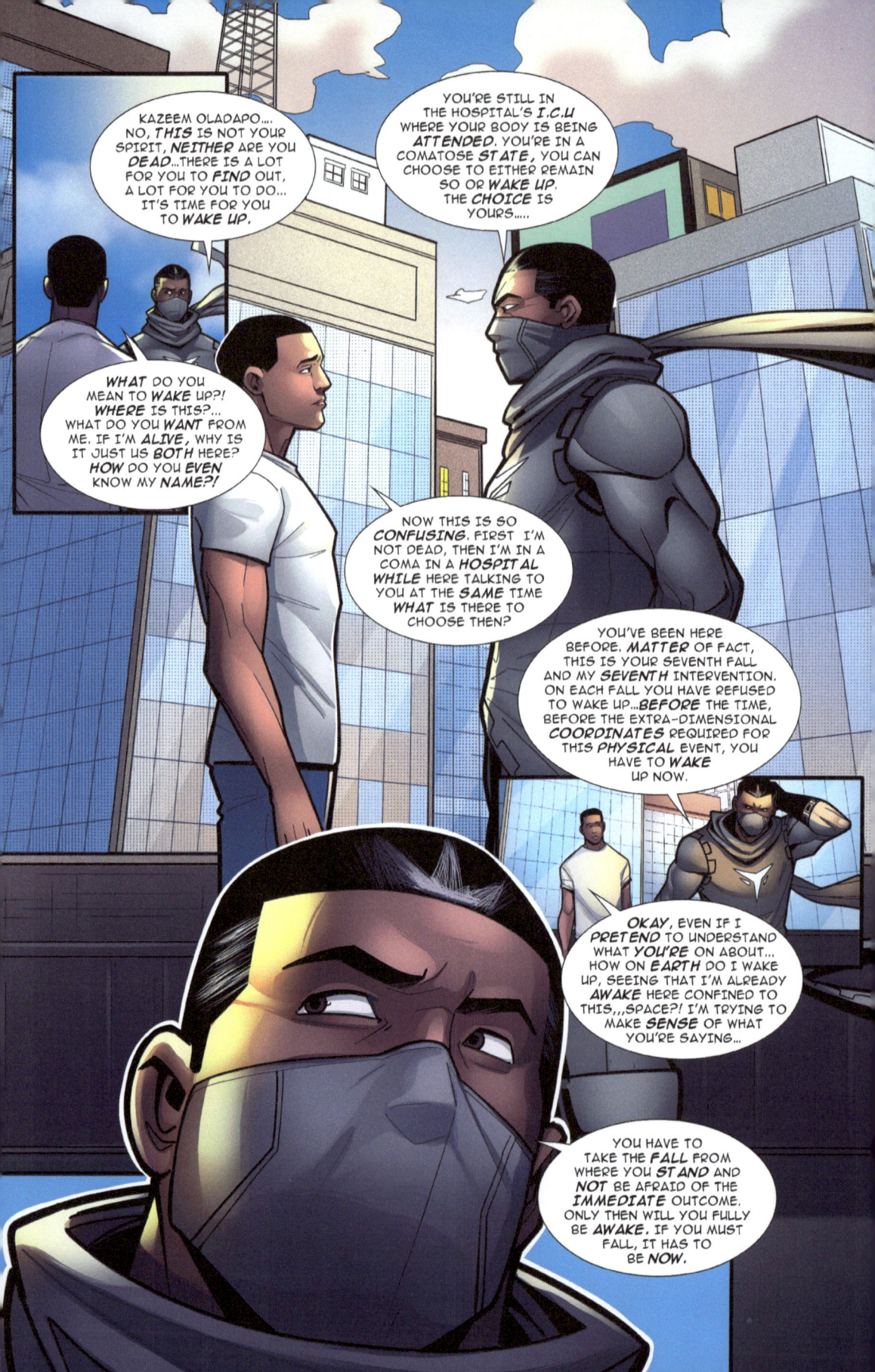

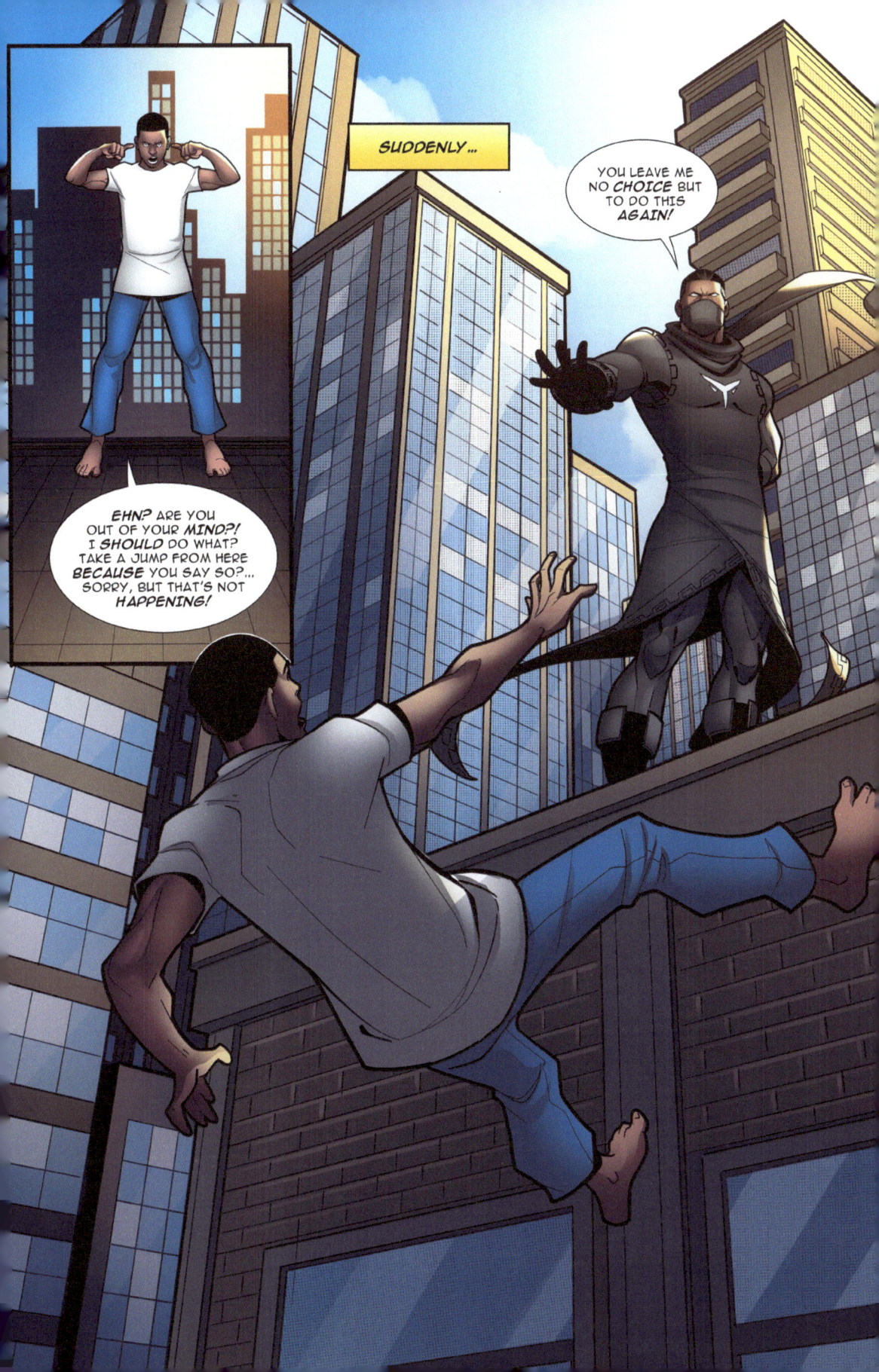

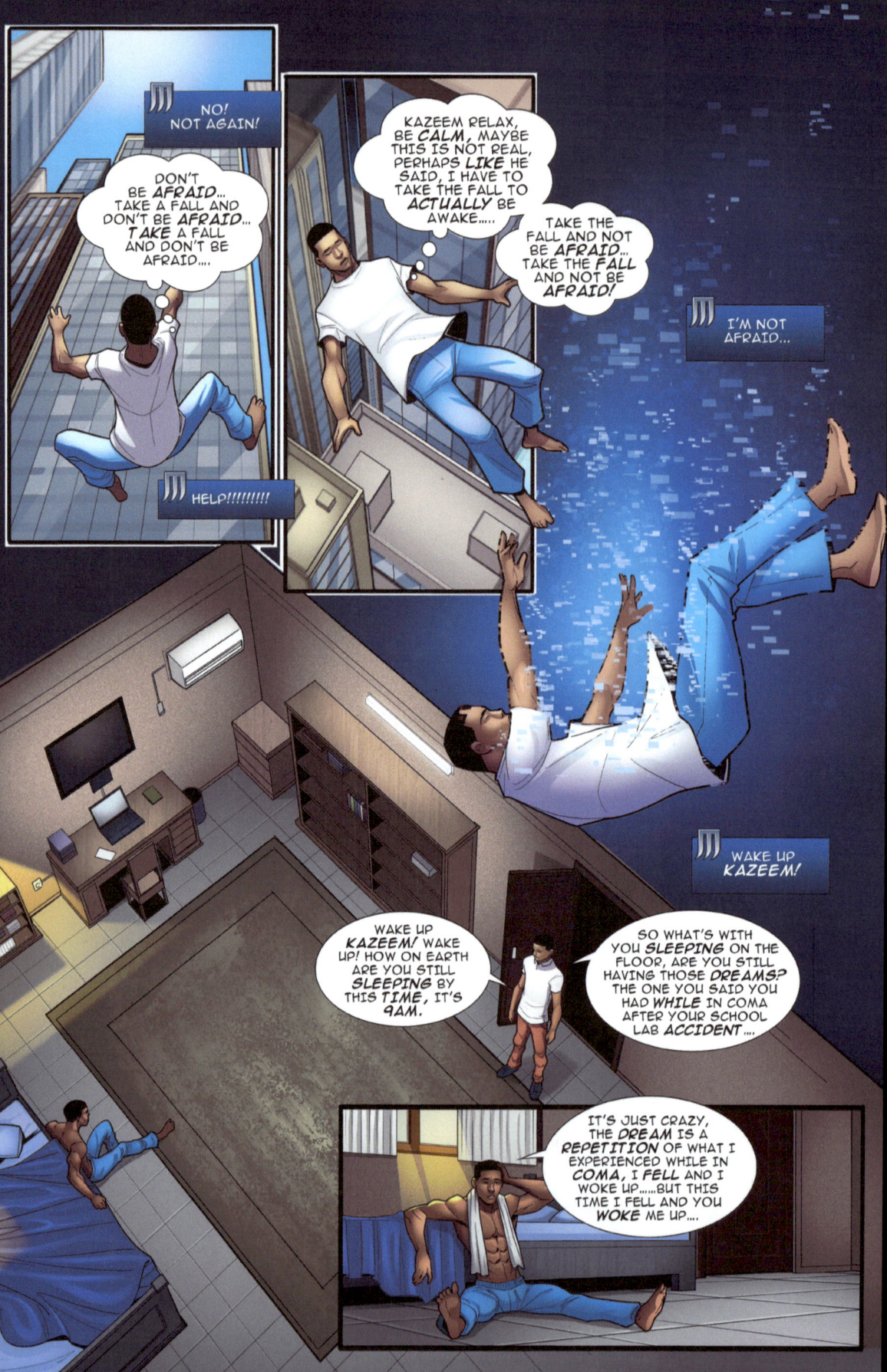

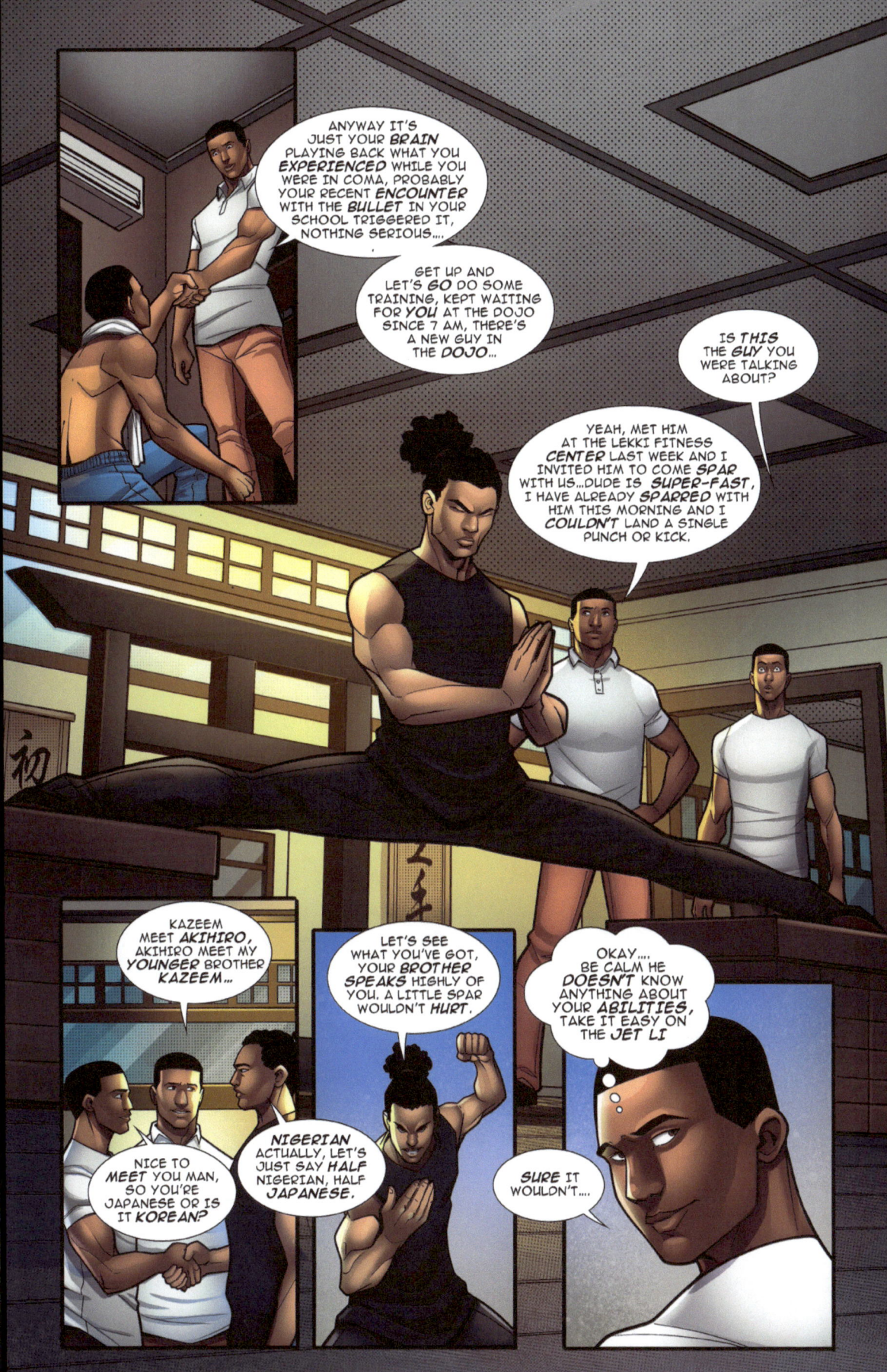

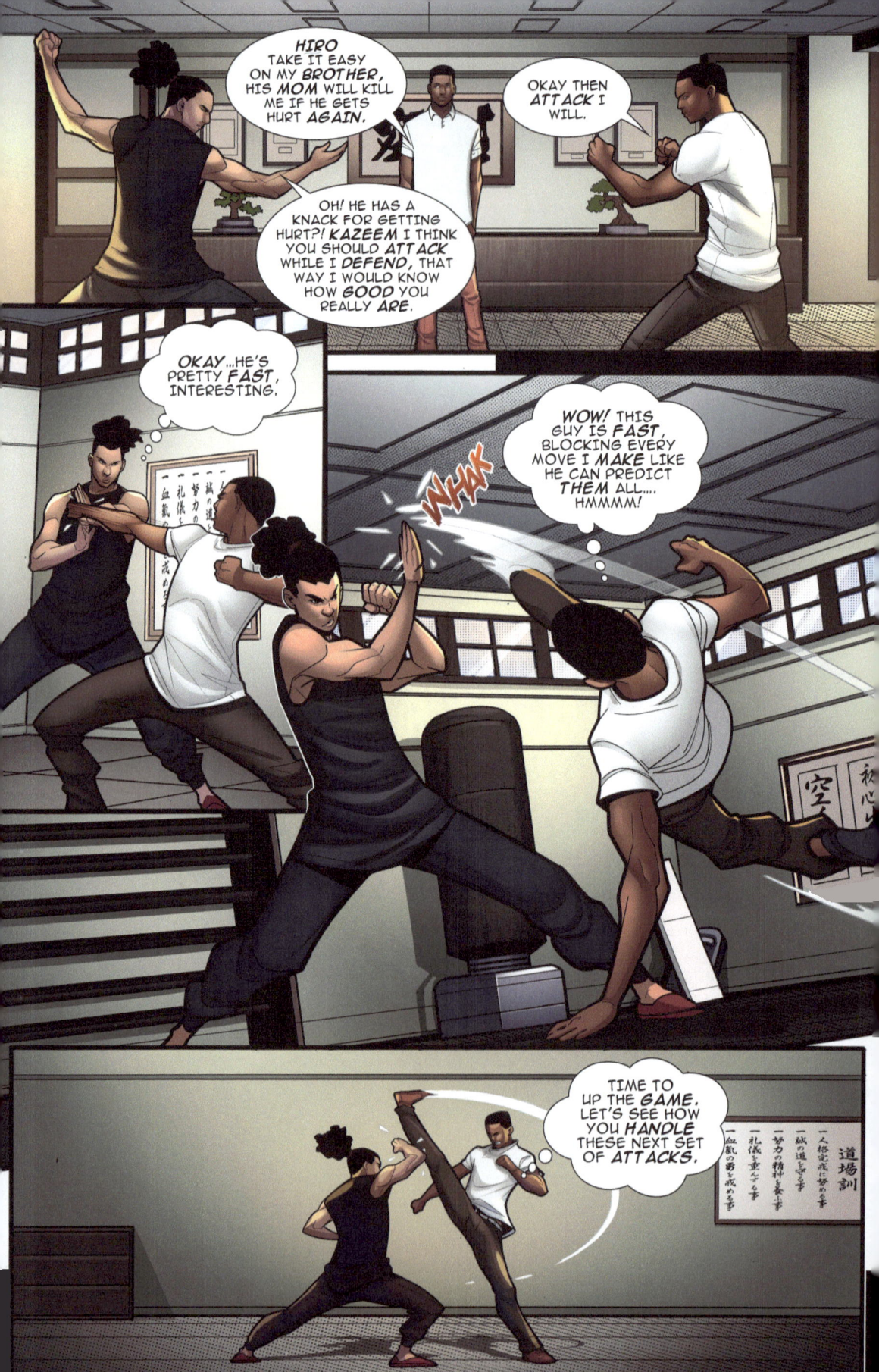

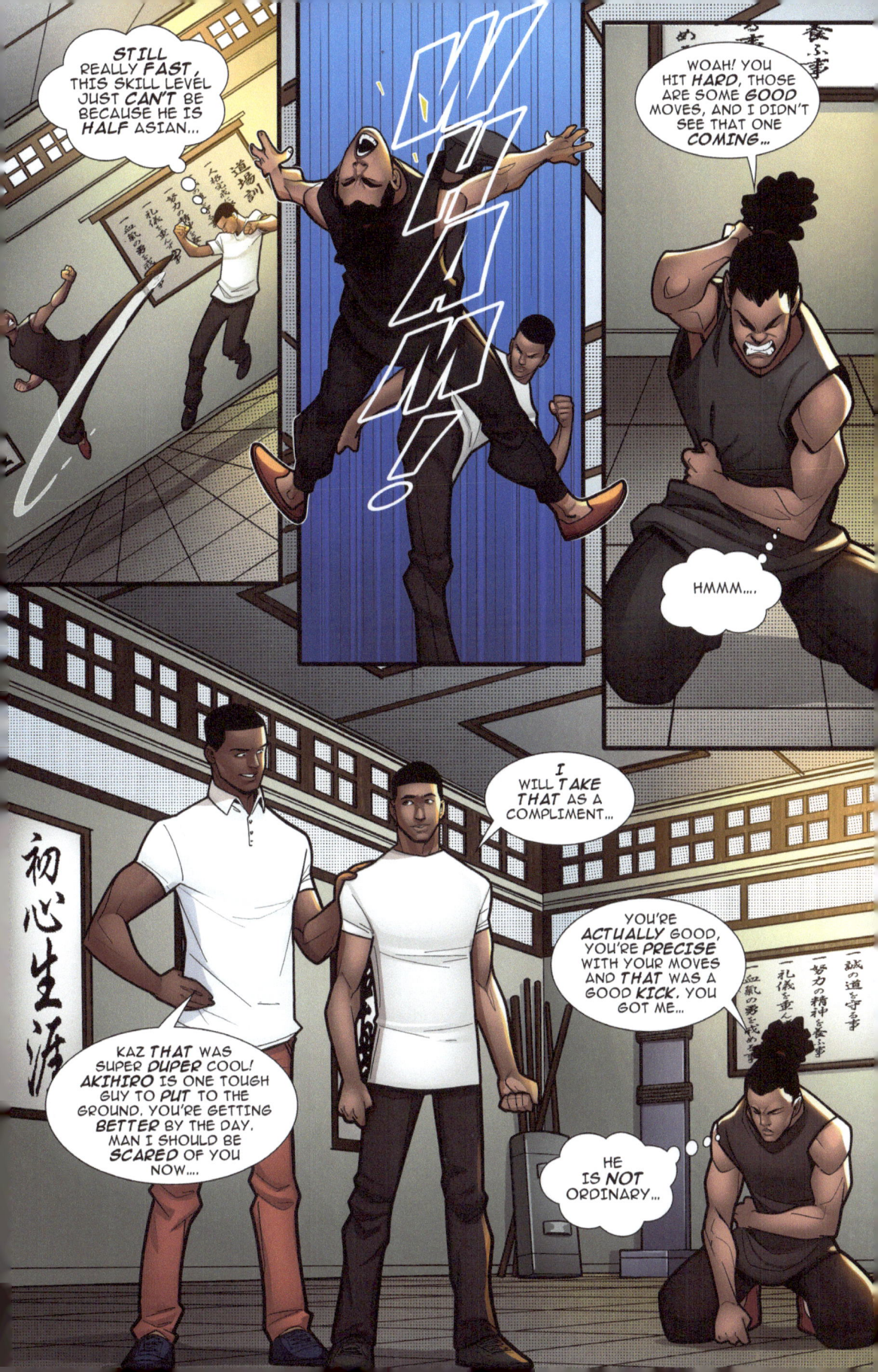

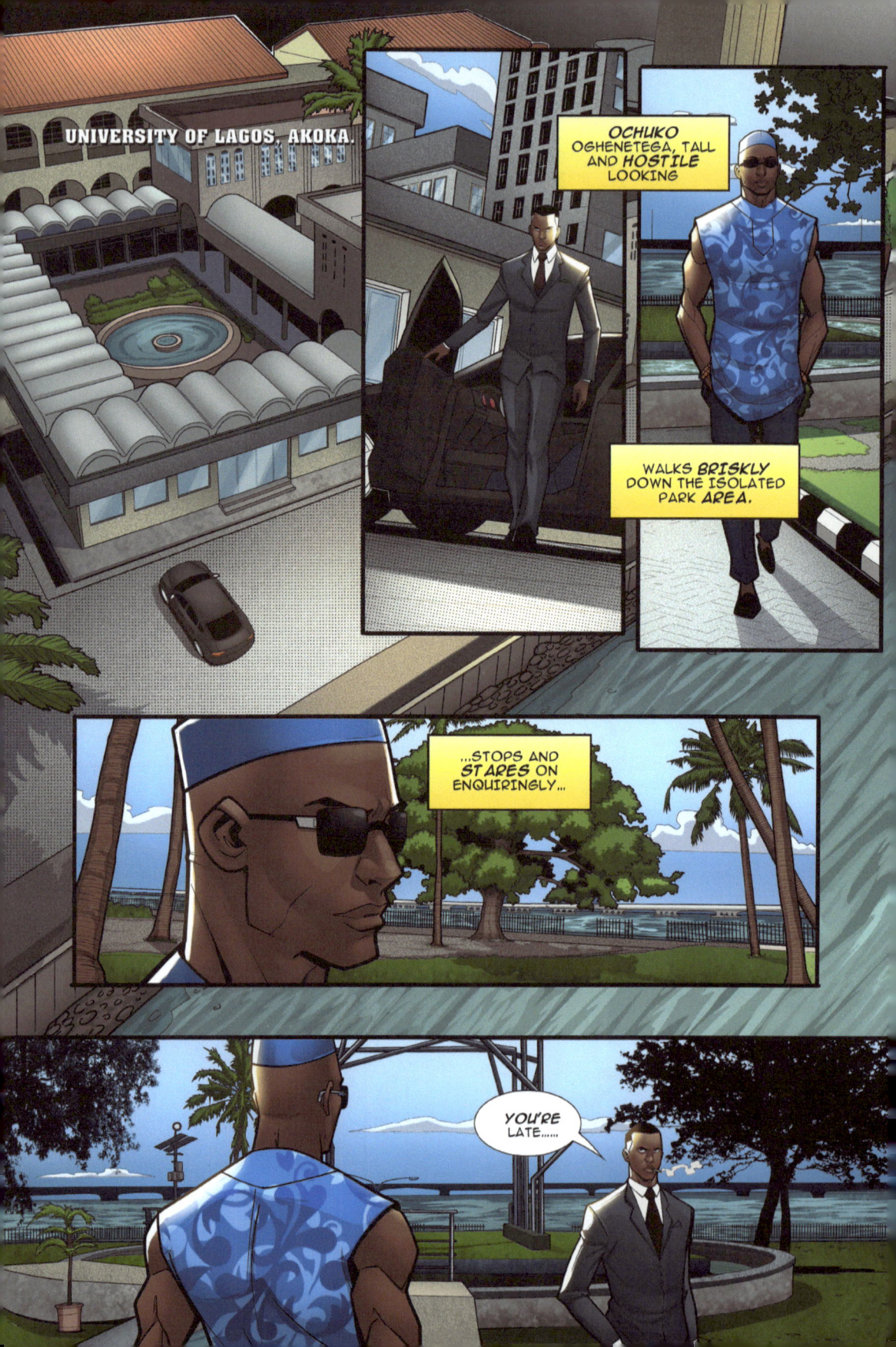

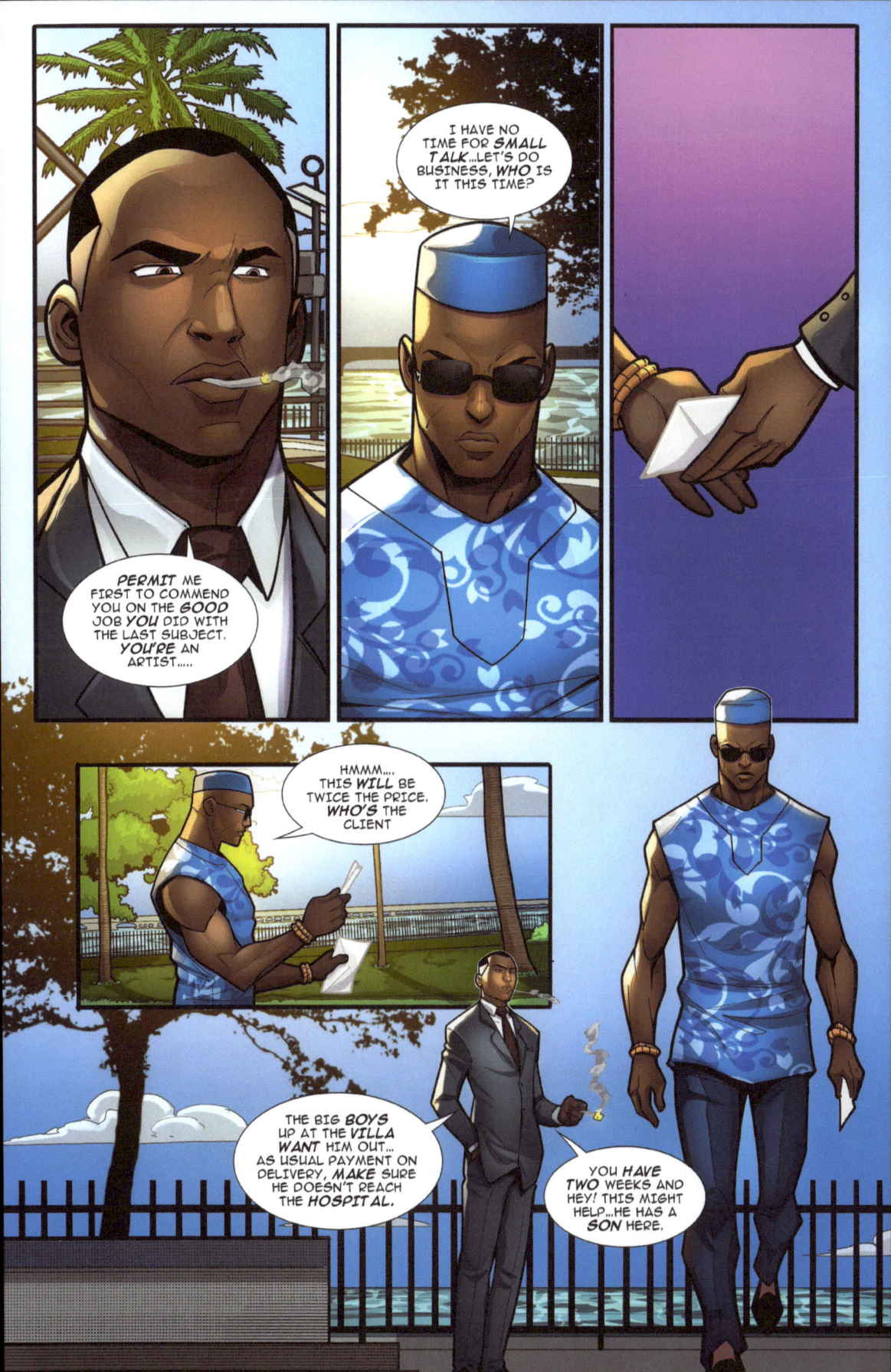

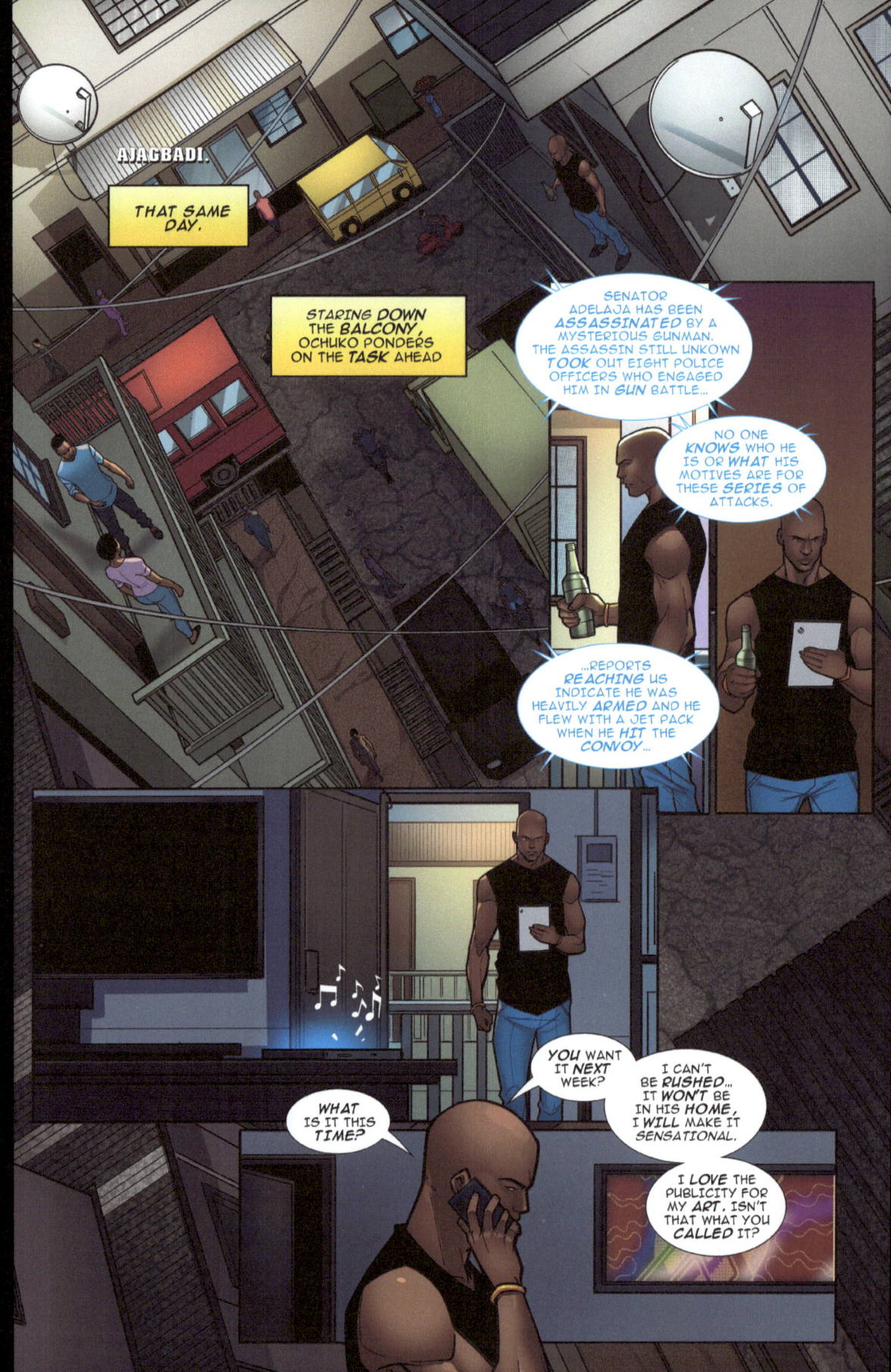

AJAGBADI.

THAT SAME DAY.

STARING *DOWN* THE *BALCONY*, OCHUKO PONDERS ON THE *TASK* AHEAD

SENATOR ADELAJA HAS BEEN *ASSASSINATED* BY A MYSTERIOUS GUNMAN. THE ASSASSIN STILL *UNKOWN* *TOOK* OUT EIGHT POLICE OFFICERS WHO ENGAGED HIM IN *GUN* BATTLE...

NO ONE *KNOWS* WHO HE IS OR *WHAT* HIS MOTIVES ARE FOR THESE *SERIES* OF ATTACKS.

...REPORTS *REACHING* US INDICATE HE WAS HEAVILY *ARMED* AND HE FLEW WITH A *JET PACK* WHEN HE *HIT* THE *CONVOY*...

YOU WANT IT *NEXT* WEEK?

I CAN'T BE *RUSHED*... IT *WON'T* BE IN HIS *HOME*, I *WILL* MAKE IT *SENSATIONAL*.

WHAT IS IT THIS *TIME?*

I *LOVE* THE PUBLICITY FOR MY *ART*. ISN'T THAT WHAT YOU *CALLED* IT?

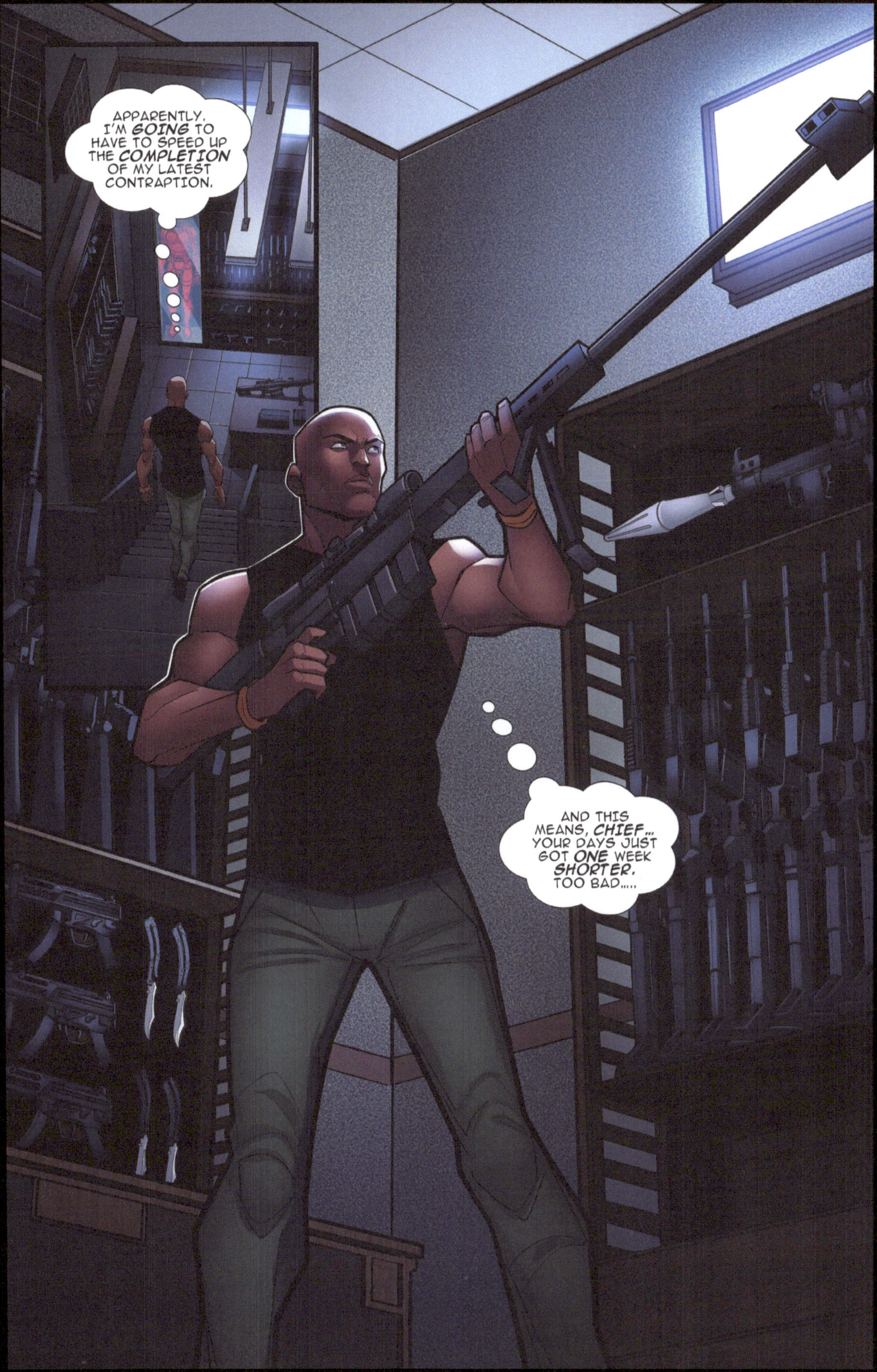
APPARENTLY, I'M GOING TO HAVE TO SPEED UP THE COMPLETION OF MY LATEST CONTRAPTION.
AND THIS MEANS, CHIEF... YOUR DAYS JUST GOT ONE WEEK SHORTER. TOO BAD.....

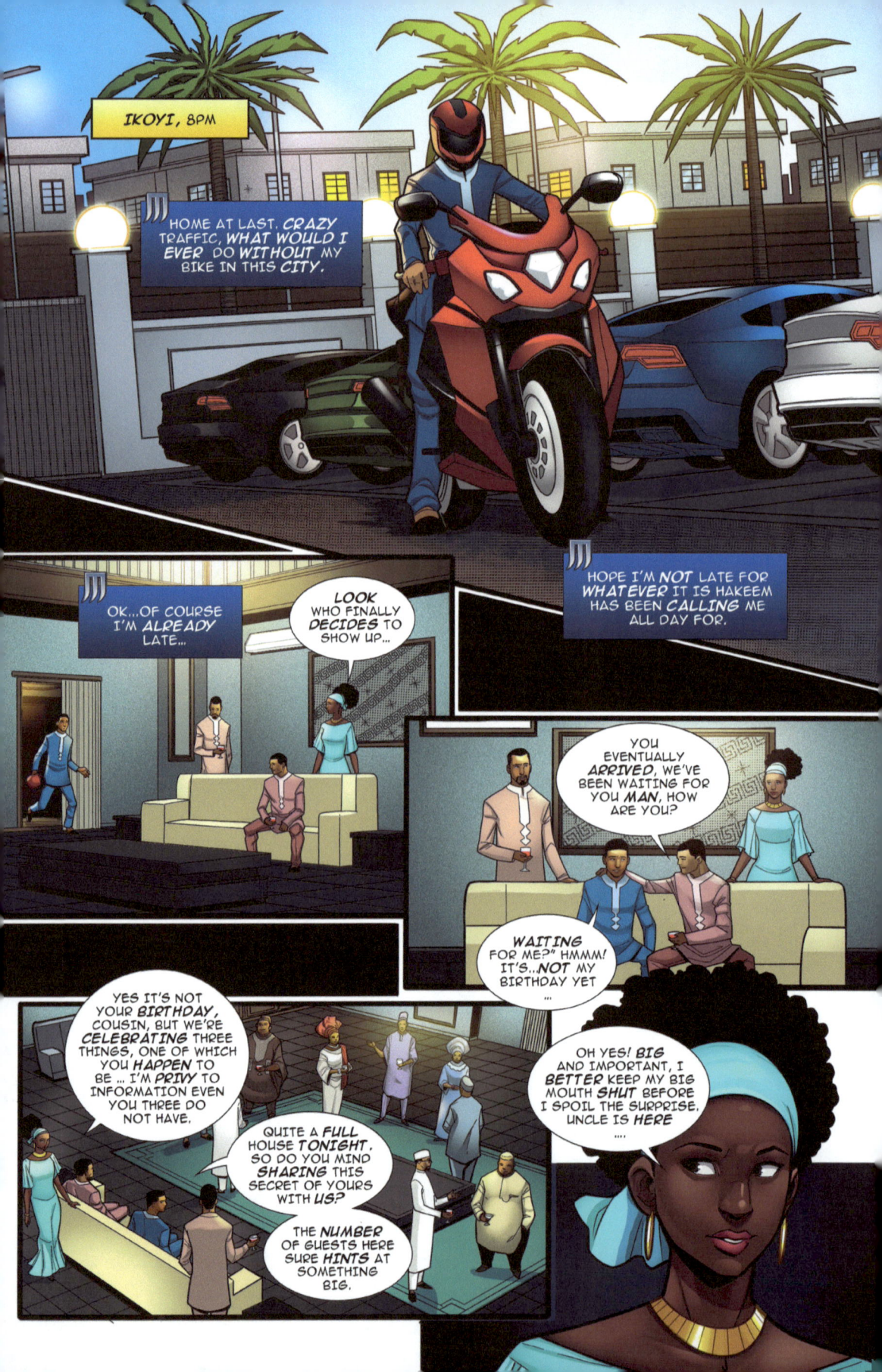

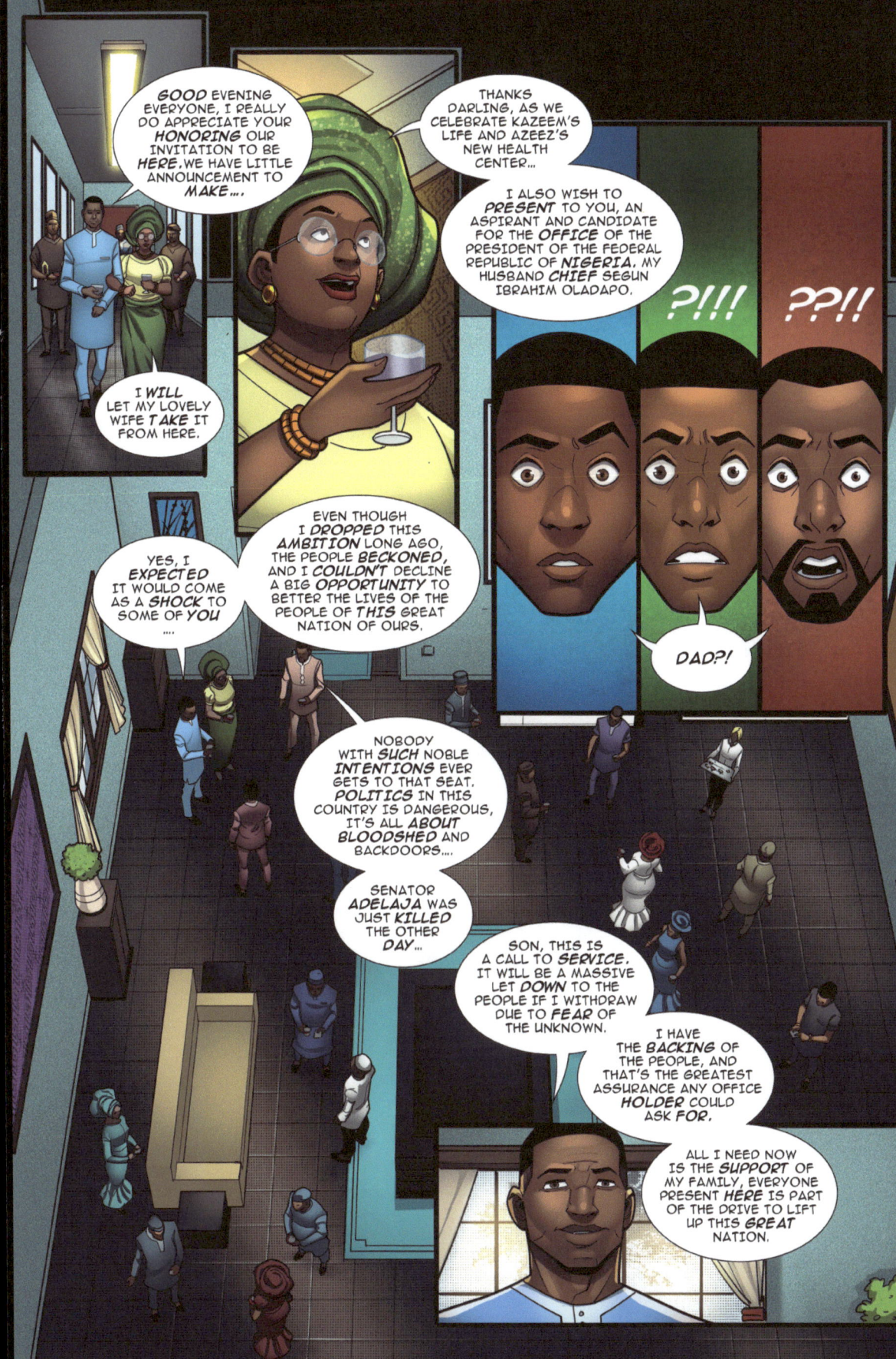

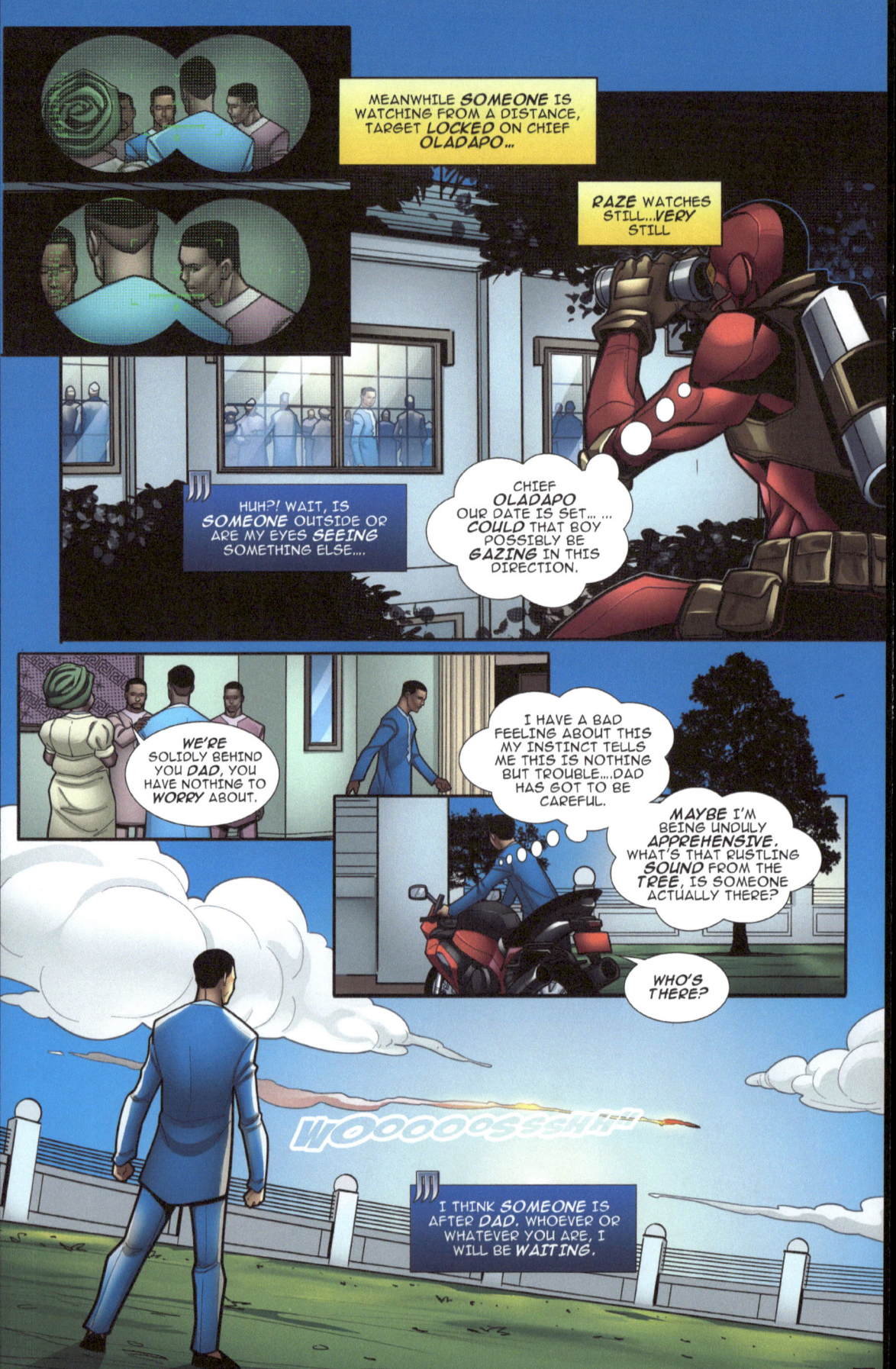

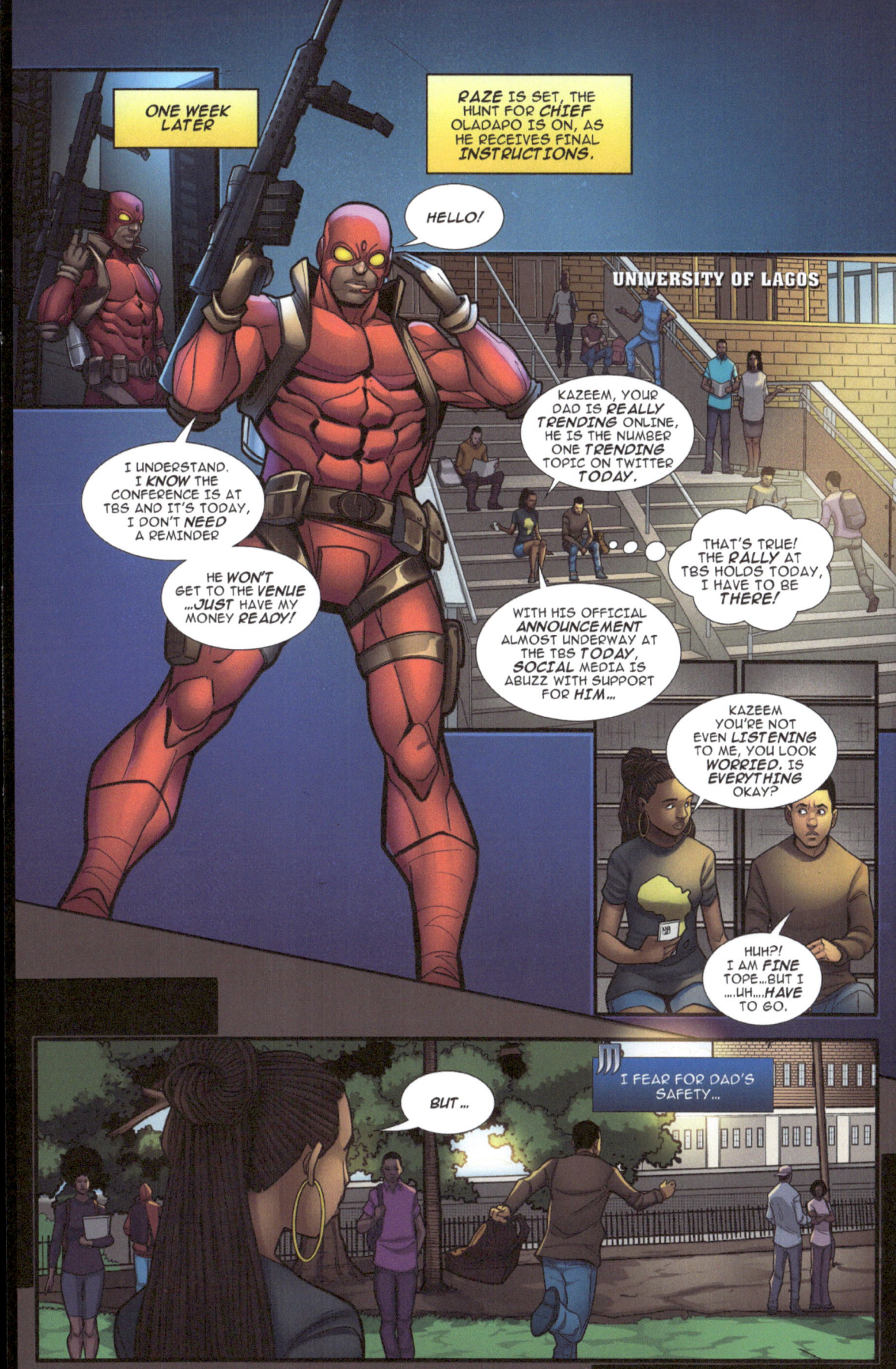

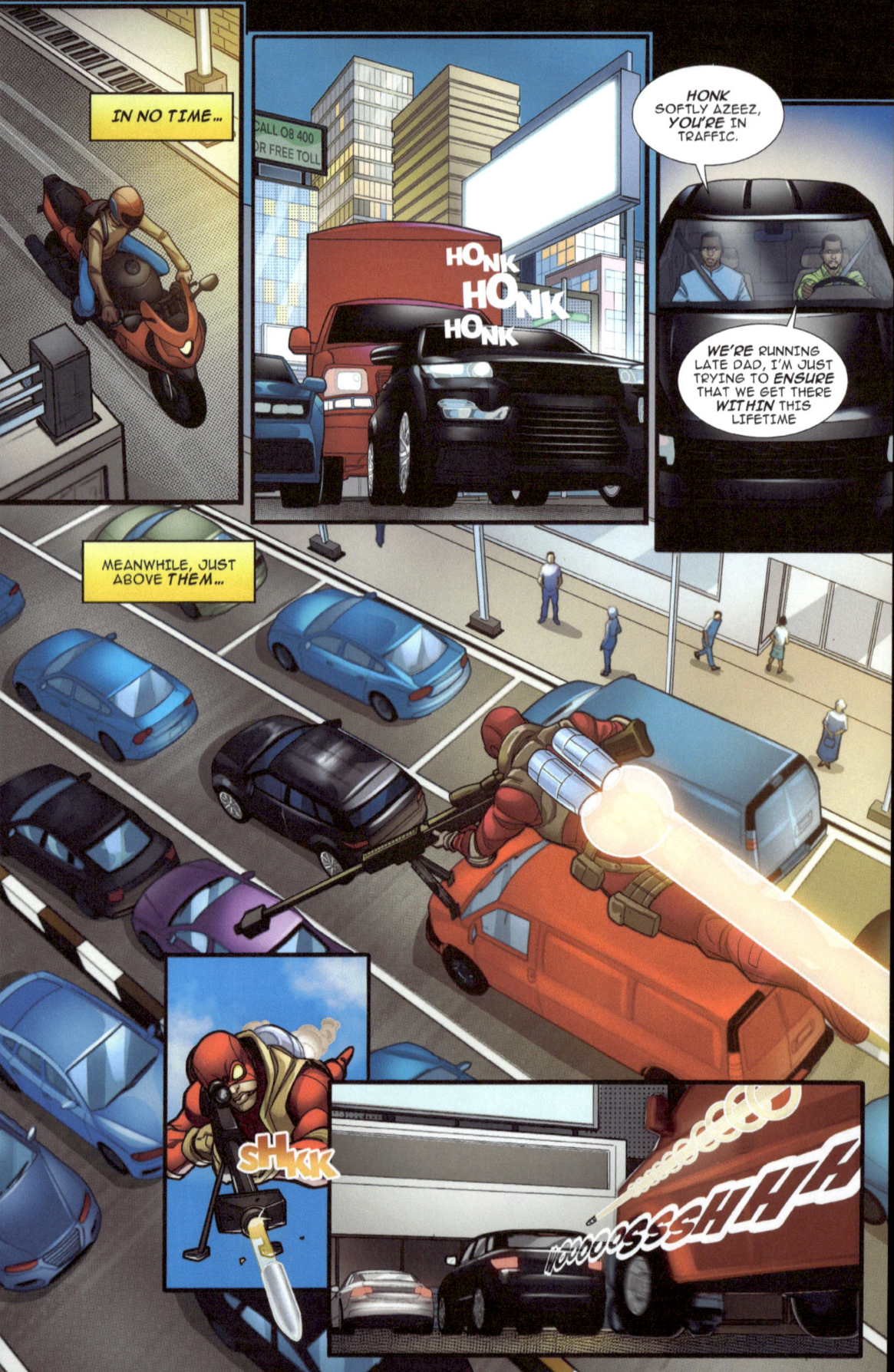

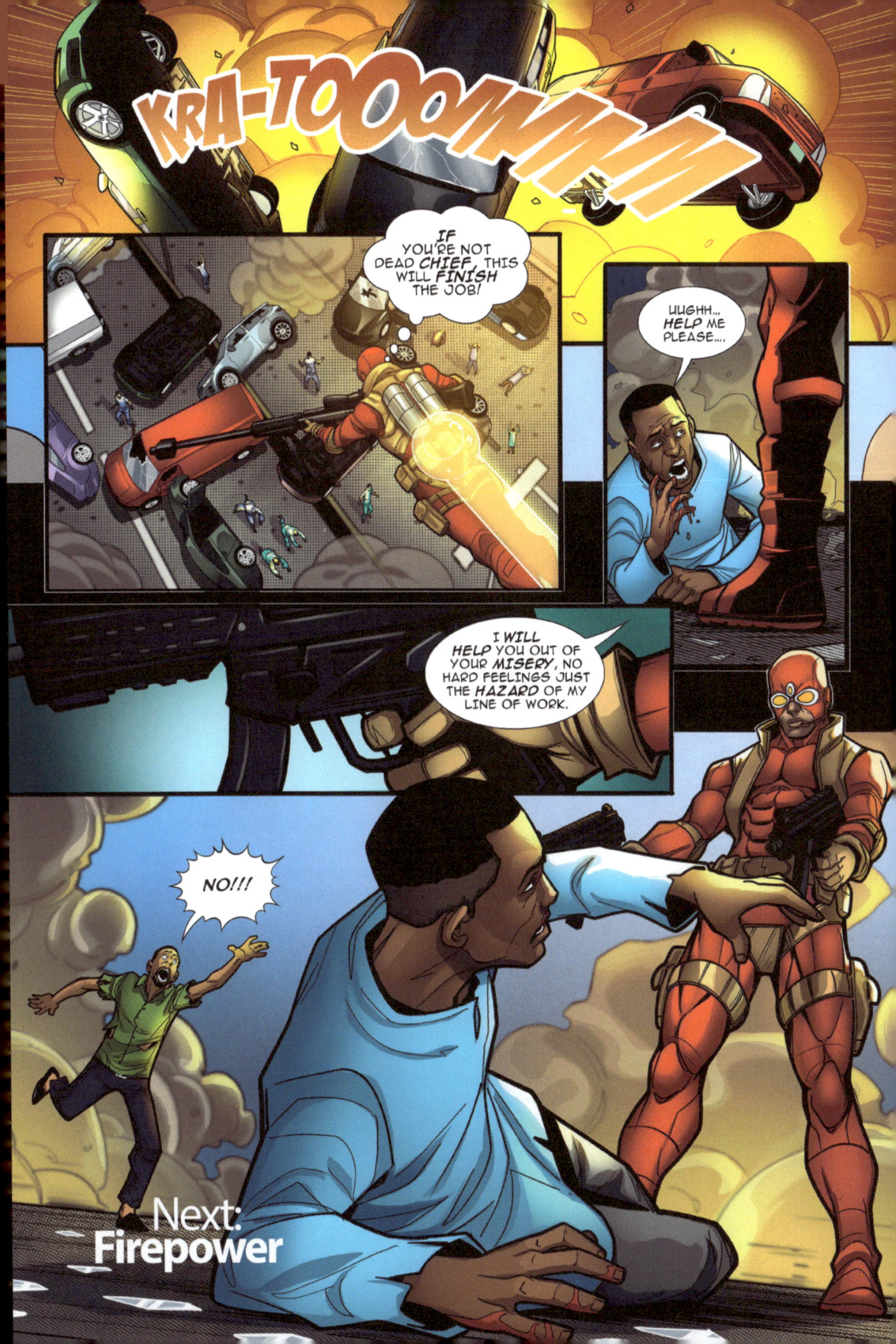

KRA-TOOOMMM

IF YOU'RE NOT DEAD *CHIEF*, THIS WILL *FINISH* THE JOB!

UUGHH... *HELP* ME PLEASE....

I WILL *HELP* YOU OUT OF YOUR *MISERY*, NO HARD FEELINGS JUST THE *HAZARD* OF MY LINE OF WORK.

NO!!!

Next:
Firepower

THE MOON FAN BASE

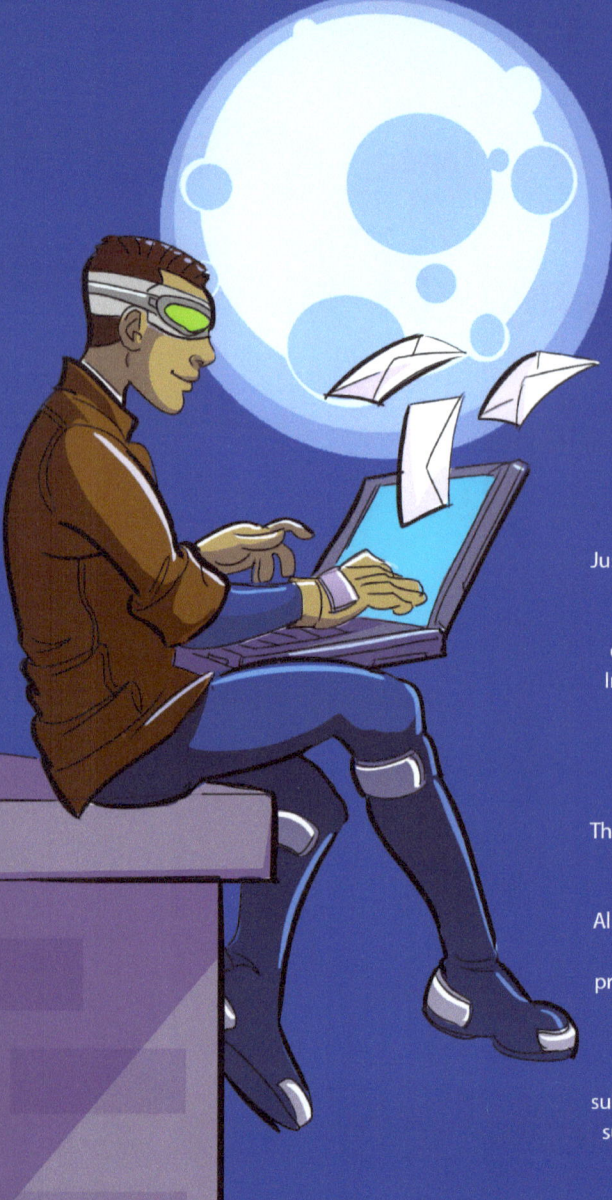

NOTE FROM THE EDITOR.

Hey!

Just like we did with Moondust #1, it also became important for us to do something about the original edition of MOONDUST #2. The art also didn't quite age well , as it was done about 20 years ago while the artist was still a student. Infact, Martin Okonkwo's daughter called out Epoch Comics for the weird looking art of that old edition. We try to maintain great quality visuals for all our projects and this is no exception. This time we featured the art of the highly talented Dominic Oziren for pencils and inks. The colourist, Abosede Akanni, (Pseudo named) is also one of the high flyers in the industry today .

Also just like the issue #1 remake, we decided not to alter the story too much, but to find ways to overlay it with the present day Epoch Universe's theme. The supernatural angle to the lab incident and the ensuing coma has finally been revealed, and we're sure you were surprised to find Sient (Dinobi Achebe) making an appearance in Kazeem's subconsious, and in this title for that matter. There'll be more surprises in issue 5, which is already in the works and will be the next instalment in the series..
See you at issue #5 and the numerous sequels to come!

Do reach us via our website or any of our social media pages below. Like, comment and share our updates. Also feel free to let us know how we can make this better because you're the reason we do it

Stay inspired!

Follow us:

f epochcomics
🐦 @epochcomics_ng
📷 @epochcomics

ENTER THE EPOCHVERSE

www.epochstudios.co

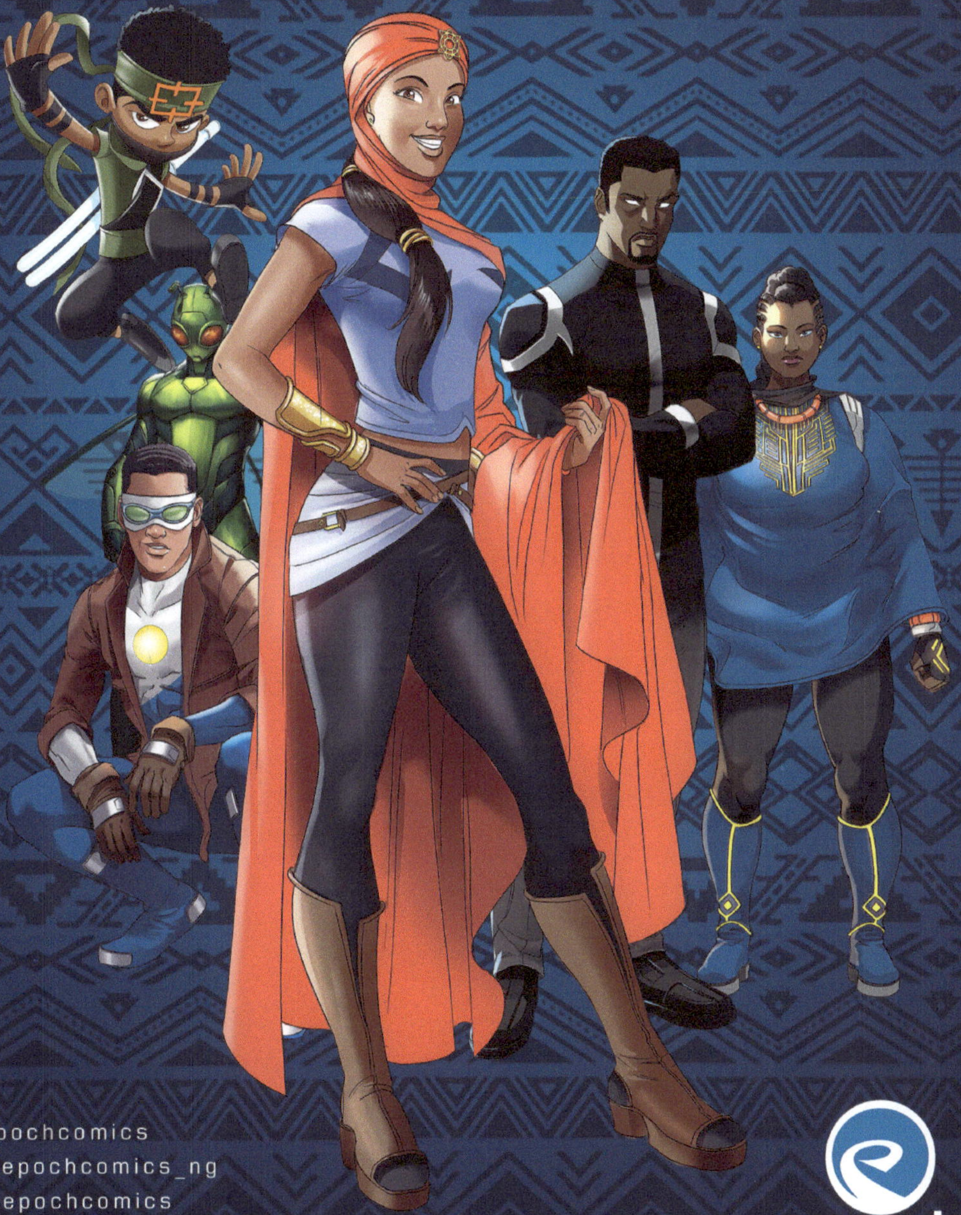

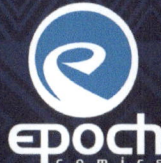